YOU DESERVE
BEAUTIFUL ROOMS

Life-Enhancing Interior Design

YOU DESERVE BEAUTIFUL ROOMS

Life-Enhancing Interior Design

Perla Lichi

Principal Photographer Barry Grossman
Principal Editor Janet Verdeguer

Published by

The
Ashley
Group

Published by

The Ashley Group

A Cahners Business Information® Company

1350 East Touhy Avenue

Des Plaines, Illinois 60018

847.390.2882   FAX 847.390.2902

Email: ashleybooksales@cahners.com

Printed in China

Concept and Design by Paul A. Casper

ISBN 1-58862-016-6

First Edition

Acknowledgments

My thanks to the homeowners who graciously allowed us to photograph their homes for use in this book. A special thanks also goes to the many talented craftsmen whose work appears in the photos, including

Mario Perger, Master Craftsman

Creative Design in Carpets

The Platt Collection

and

very special thanks to

Paul McRae, The Galleria Collection of Fine Homes

Contents

Introduction

At a very early age, I knew that I would become an interior designer. My parents are in the jewelry business and exposure to both sides – the aesthetics of the product and the business of making a profit – were always part of daily life. Mother tells me that I always wanted to reorganize the display cases because I knew instinctively how they should be arranged to best advantage. Then, as a precocious teen, I worked in the store and became one of the star salespeople, never afraid to tell clients which earrings, necklaces, or broaches they should or should not wear.

From this early "space planning" experience, I went on to earn my degree in interior design and started working as a staff designer for several well-established firms. If anything, I am a true daughter of Aries – impetuous and ambitious – and it wasn't long before having my own company became my goal. Perla Lichi Design was founded in 1990, and in the first decade my business has grown to dominance in South Florida.

We are now beginning to expand to other geographical areas as well. The main ingredient for my success, I believe, is that I look at design differently than most of my colleagues do. I am passionate about it. I love it. I live it day in and day out. And I truly believe that good design enhances daily life – in every way. But due to my early experience, I also know that design is a business. Successful design is the result of education combined with practical experience. Designers do not need special protection for their profession nor are they somehow "above the fray." This becomes especially clear to me on those less-than-glamorous days when I am schlepping lamps and furniture in 90-degree South Florida heat on a job site with no air-conditioning!

If anything, at this mid-stage of my career, I'm more open than ever. I believe that the more I share about what I do and why, the more importance design will have in the eyes of those around me, and ultimately, in the eyes of the world.

This book is divided into 10 chapters, starting with design guidelines in regards to color, personality, collections, etc. Then I provide some insight into matching your personality with your interiors, including information available through astrology. The rest of the book presents installations and actual case studies of particular clients, with valuable information about the investment value of professional interior design.

As 2000 dawned, my dream of having my own syndicated newspaper column became a reality with the launch of The Decor Diva®. We are now reaching more than five million readers in 14 cities. The Decor Diva®, "the interior design answer lady," is me. My philosophy that it is better to have a happy life than a life "style" stands firm. I think you will find that this book represents a fresh look at interior design. It comes from my heart because I truly believe that you – yes, you! – deserve beautiful rooms.

– Perla Lichi

Interior Design and You

The Decor Diva's First Commandment: Enjoy Your Life!

How the interior of your home looks is a very personal matter.

Although there are many basic rules and technical aspects that apply to sound principles of interior design, when it comes to residential interiors, the home should reflect its owner's own personality. Yes, it is important to have correct space planning, the right color coordination, balance and harmony. But, as the old adage says, "beauty is in the eye of the beholder."

Even the untrained eye, however, can easily distinguish professionally planned and executed interiors from those created by do-it-yourselfers. It may not recognize exactly why one look is "better" than another, but it is aware that something about the scene is desirable. Yet most people are still reticent about getting professional guidance in this important area of their lives. Why? Over the years I have been confronted with many objections, and the first is almost always cost.

People perceive that a designer is an unnecessary expense for a service they believe they can easily accomplish themselves by visiting a few stores and showrooms. In other words they do not "value" this service enough to put a price tag on it. When you think about it, it is rather interesting that the expenditure of $30 or $40 thousand dollars for a new car — not only once in their lives but every few years — is considered the norm. Yet making this type of investment for beautiful home interiors still raises eyebrows.

There are also the secondary fears: that a designer will impose his or her own personal tastes or hard sell them products they don't really want or need. Many people are also intimidated and even somewhat embarrassed to open their most private spaces to the scrutiny of a total stranger. The good news is that more people are learning about the benefits of working with an interior designer. Design and shelter magazines have done a great job by presenting well designed interiors and sources, crediting professionals and identifying their input. Word-of-mouth has also helped, as one person in a neighborhood has a good experience and shares it with a friend or neighbor. A goal of this book is to demonstrate how beautiful, well planned interiors are a sound investment, not only in the quality of your life but also in the value of your home.

How many of us really have the time to spend researching the proper materials, keeping up with the latest technological developments and style trends? This is a designer's day-to-day job. Then there is the time spent buying, scheduling installations, preparation and clean-up, not to mention trouble-shooting the inevitable problems and coordinating these steps in an orderly fashion from beginning to end.

"The good news is that more people are learning about the benefits of working with an interior designer."

15

"Beautiful, well-planned interiors are a sound investment, not only in the quality of your life but also in the value of your home."

"Freedom of design is your ultimate goal, and this freedom will convert an area of concern in your life into one of supreme enjoyment."

"Interior design is not an area of mystery. It can be a pleasant experience that will enhance your life and that of your loved ones for many, many years."

An interview with Thomas Stanley, author of The Millionaire Mind (Andrews McMeel, 2000) indicates self-made millionaires don't like do-it-yourself repairs: "Wealthy people are smart about saying, 'What is the value of the time it would take me to paint my house? It might save me a few thousand dollars, but I could play four rounds of golf in the same time it would take me to paint my home, and I could do it with people who are prospective clients or current clients or suppliers.'" (The interview is by Susan Garland in the July-August 2000 issue of Modern Maturity.)

There are many advantages to working with a designer. No more plodding through home improvement and hardware stores or taking do-it-yourself courses in the art of setting ceramic tile. No more crash courses in the intricacies of selecting and installing window rods. Best of all — no more costly mistakes or embarrassment when you see your results are less than your expectations.

A good way to begin — even before you speak with a designer — is to gather magazines and pull out the pages of those interiors that get your attention. Any time that you see something you like in a magazine, rip it out and begin to build a portfolio of ideas. Arranged by room or topic in a notebook, these tears sheets will come in handy as you design your home, creating an invaluable reference that will help you understand your personal preferences and define them for others. So what if some of your choices are contemporary while some are traditional? If you like it, pull it! Later, you will see how the most beautiful interiors are eclectic and timeless. Freedom of design is your ultimate goal, and this freedom will convert an area of concern into one of supreme enjoyment.

Yes. My first advice is for you to relax and enjoy your life — including your decorating projects. Keep in mind that a designer can be hired to plan a single project or handle every intricate detail of an entire home renovation. And even though you are not on "Who Wants to Be a Millionaire," there are many, many lifelines along the way. Interior design is not an area of mystery. It can be a pleasant experience that will enhance your life for many, many years. You deserve beautiful rooms.

Assessing Your Design Personality

Most people don't realize that their home always reflects their personality. The minute you walk into a home specific things will tend to stand out above others: the type of books on the shelves, the number of framed paintings on the walls, or even something as specific as the particular types of frames around the artwork. These choices are revealing. Color selection also speaks volumes about the individual, as does the style of the furnishings. Other indicators come from their sense of organization (or lack thereof) and how well everything flows.

Personality! Yes, that is what sets you apart from everyone else and you should always feel free to express yourself in your own personal space. The most obvious indicators of personality are color, collections, and style.

color

Most people tend to be very consistent in both the way they dress and in the way they decorate their homes. Bright colors represent sharp, open, high-energy people who like to be noticed and do not want to blend with the background. Their home will reflect the same energies. I always recommend bright colors for accessories such as accent pillows or artwork that can be easily changed.

Primary colors of red, blue, and yellow are used in very high-tech designs or in children's rooms. These are great attention getters when applied to artwork and accessories and can also be used as accent walls for a most dramatic statement. Secondary colors of green, purple and orange are also great accent colors for contemporary interiors, and juvenile rooms. Adding white to them results in beautiful shades of lavender, peach and soft green, which are easily used in more traditional rooms.

Then you have "cool" and "hot" colors. Reds are hot, blues are cool.

In my experience, the cool colors such as blues, turquoises, aquas, lavenders, periwinkles, and any mix of color with the blue/cool shades appeal to those who prefer a soothing, relaxed atmosphere. These colors can be used as accents or as backgrounds. The hot/warm colors — variances of reds, pinks, burgundies, wines, apricots, salmons, and any color where the red pigment is dominant — tend to stimulate excitement more so than the cool colors. To achieve balance between "hot" and "cool" these colors can be combined within the same room resulting in a beautiful look. It is suggested to balance them if you can, but it is also okay if you do not. This brings me back to the fact that unconsciously your taste and your choice of color will reflect your personality as well as set the ambiance you so desire. Last but certainly not least are the earth tones, colors that create a sense of

"Unconsciously your taste and your choice
of color will reflect your personality as well as set the ambiance you so desire."

harmony in your interiors by bringing nature indoors. Mother Nature herself decorated our world in colors that are eternal, timeless, never "trendy" yet always in style.

Examples from today's palette include bones, creams, taupes, camels, browns, burnt sienna, sage green, and eggplant—all inspired by nature and all considered "warm." These colors will tend to create a monochromatic palette in which texture becomes more important as a decorating element. A blend of textures compliments the earth tones and creates pleasure to the eye as well as to the touch.

Natural materials of granite, marble and stone are also desirable complements. And let's not forget wood, a natural material that is essential in almost every design scheme.

Keep the larger fields of color in a neutral palette. Then bring in whatever colors attract you as accents. Buy that purple sofa or red chair, if that is what turns you on, but always aim for balance by introducing other accents of this color in your accessories. If your personality is bold, then be bold in your decor. If you are calm and serene, then that is what you should seek in your personal surroundings.

"If your personality is bold, then be bold in your decor. If you are calm and serene, then that is what you should seek in your personal surroundings."

collections

Family heirlooms, specialized collections, items collected from around the world over a lifetime ... these really imbue your home with personality. My advice: use them, use them, and use them! I have heard of decorators who have actually left people in tears by advising them to give away their collectibles. I say, get rid of that decorator and use these items to make your home unique and beautiful.

There are many ways to display collections effectively and enhance the design of your home, and the key is not to scatter but to group them. If they are small items, that is all the more reason to group them.

"There are many ways to display collections effectively and enhance the design of your home."

My clients were retiring and relocating from New York with their priceless collection of antique clocks. They also had a number of Erte sculptures. Although he was in the process of parting with some of these clocks by having them auctioned at Sotheby's, he still wanted to display around 150 of them in his new home. We built special display cases in three different rooms and used some of the more spectacular ones as accent accessories. The result was magnificent.

The buzzword for interior design during the 1980s was "matching." Today, thankfully, we're not "matching," we're "blending." And believe me, blending is better.

One of the biggest "design" crimes committed by this fixation on "matching" was the loss of

"Everything that comes from nature
is already naturally coordinated.
Look at the trees in the forest,
hundreds of varieties, and they look just fine together,
don't they?"

the individuality of the homeowner. The wonderful personal aspect is, after all, what truly makes a house a home, and it was being consciously erased for the sake of "design." Beautiful, hand-done marquetry should not be painted over to "match" the rest of the furnishings. A wonderful mahogany writing desk, a family heirloom, with a patina developed over the years, should be prominently displayed.

Today, fortunately, these rigid regulations have faded. People recognize benefits of good design that reach well beyond the glitz, or the stiffness of trying to match everything. I think this is due to the plethora of design magazines and cable television shows that have heightened awareness of what good design really is. People are also traveling to different parts of the world and widening their exposure to new and diverse schools of design.

Today people are looking for more than color coordination. They are seeking peace and comfort that comes from being surrounded with elements of good design. Many schools of design have come and gone during the last few centuries, and new styles are constantly emerging. Rooms can be painstakingly recreated in any period style. Would you like to duplicate what Louis XV did in the Palace of Versailles? You would probably find this just a bit too stuffy and formal.

"Today people are looking for more than color coordination. They are seeking peace and comfort that comes from being surrounded with elements of good design."

And why not bring Louis XVI in too? Who says we can't mix both? And don't forget Napoleon and the Empire style introduced during his time. And this is only the French Classics. We can't overlook the English styles, including Queen Anne, and the many different styles that later emerged such as Chippendale, Hepplewhite, and so forth. The Bauhaus movement at the dawn of the 20th century segued into Modernism in the 1930s. And on and on.

The truth of the matter is that we are now living in the 21st century. Past centuries had their own design problems and their solutions of the day certainly do not reflect our contemporary needs or lifestyles.

But there is no reason we can't have a touch of past styles or elegance incorporated into our lifestyle and home. I frequently go back in time even further, architecturally combining styles dating from the Greeks and later the Romans. Why not? Be eclectic and you will never be out of style.

Color coordination is very important when mixing styles. Let's say you find two beautiful Louis XVI Bergere chairs. Add a distressed or crackle finish so that they look really old. Then select a fabric that will flow with the rest of your furnishings. A beautiful tapestry fabric would be a

"Be eclectic and you will never be out of style."

good choice with your colors incorporated into the pattern. Keep the sofa in a textured neutral or in a color that appears somewhere within the woven tapestry design. Add several accent pillows in the tapestry with a bullion fringe and throw these on the sofa. It should look like the pillows are growing out of the sofa with newly emerged colors within. Yes! That's it! Now I'm really getting inspired!

Astrology Lends a Helping Hand

Another Guide to Discovering the True You

I was born on the same date as Renaissance artist and inventor Leonardo da Vinci and have always considered him to be my kindred spirit. My accomplishments certainly can't compare with those of the renowned Florentine painter, sculptor, architect and engineer. This shared birth date does, I think, explain my lifelong tendency to be intensely curious about how things work, and also to be very creative.

While I have definitely noticed the influence of my sign (Aries) on my life, and diligently read my horoscope every day, I also realize many find belief in the Zodiac to be mere folklore. In both my professional and personal life, however, it has increasingly come to my attention that this philosophy does bring some important insight toward understanding human nature. More importantly for this book, this insight is helpful in determining a selection of home furnishings.

In this chapter I have outlined a few fundamental characteristics of the 12 signs of the Zodiac. This is just a basic overview of Sun signs. Be aware that rising signs and chart placement of planets will give you a much more accurate description. The sign associated with your Fourth House is especially important to characteristics regarding hearth and home. This is how a person sees himself, and this view manifests itself in his surroundings. You may be a Virgo (born between August and September) for example, but the sign in your Fourth House could be Leo and seemingly opposite traits can appear.

There is much positive information available through astrology for your life and your decorating needs. To understand what the astrologer is telling you about yourself and your needs, you often have to strip away the jargon that astrologers use. Imagine that an astrologer is a wise old friend who has known you and your family, even your grandparents and parents, all of your lives. You come to this counselor for advice. The "friend" will look at all aspects of your life before replying. If the friend says to you, "The planet Mars is in your Fourth House with Cancer, so you need to ...," most of us hear something like "the big rock near Jupiter has a disease in the fourth place you lived in." However, we would all understand if the friend had said, "Your desire for action finds special expression through your home and living situation. You are particularly attracted to creating a safe environment, a place where you can withdraw and rest." Each of us has desires (planets) and we have areas of our lives where these desires are most easily expressed (houses). The way in which we express these desires (quickly, smoothly, quietly, with a big bang, with a subtle touch) are the "signs" that the astrologer talks about.

Why do I often use astrology to determine what my clients will or will not like? Because it is a shortcut. If you know yourself very well or if you have a friend who knows you very well, you don't need astrology. I like to use it as a tool to assist me in knowing my clients' special, unspoken needs.

Aries

(March 21-April 19)

Planet: Mars, god of war (desire to act and initiate)
Metal: Iron
Base Element: Fire
Scent: Citrus, pine and aloe
Color: The entire red spectrum
Stone: Diamond

The child born under the sign of Aries has a clear sense of his own independence and needs to be surrounded by bright colors that help him express his uniqueness. His planet is Mars, the warrior, and he is motivated to activate, move forward, and delegate.

A very serious, formal entryway usually distinguishes an Aries home. Inside, his choice will probably include furniture made from chrome or natural fibers because he likes the discipline of the straight, clean lines. But he also has a soft side because pleasure is fundamental, and velvet or chenille upholstery with loose cushions and soft area rugs would be typical expressions of this desire.

If Cancer is in the Fourth house, the Aries will likely enjoy being in the kitchen, an area that Cancer rules. This Aries will also share a preference for heirlooms and antiques — which is a complete yet pleasing contrast to the hard-edged, contemporary lines usually preferred.

Iron furniture is always part of the Aries decorating scheme. Look for metallic-looking fabrics or fabrics with metallic threads. Fanatics about sports, another gift from energetic Mars, the Aries will want an exercise room or at least a place dedicated to exercise equipment.

Taurus

(April 20-May 20)

Planet: Venus, goddess of love (desire for harmony and stability)
Metal: Copper
Base Element: Earth
Scent: Florals: Rose, daffodil and hyacinth
Color: Earthtones
Stone: Agate with earthtones and emerald

Taurus is a detail-oriented creature who loves to be surrounded by comfortable pieces that almost never change. These same characteristics reflect his calm and peaceful demeanor. Once provoked, however, the Taurus has a red-hot temper that can erupt like a time bomb.

Conscious of his potential explosive nature, the Taurus always tries to preserve tranquility. For this reason, he prefers home furnishings in soft tones, with rich, earth tones as background since Earth is his element.

His furniture will have rounded edges such as big, comfy, soft, sturdy armchairs. His home needs to be a place where possessions can be stored safely. Since Taurus has an almost compulsive desire to collect, he is particularly interested in shelves, drawers, and armoires! He loves dinners around a large dining room table and well-stocked kitchen cabinets. A large refrigerator would also be a natural part of his home.

With the Fourth House in Leo, Taurus likes to cultivate his own private space, and there - he is king! Don't try to touch his precious things because Taurus won't allow it. Leo gives Taurus one more characteristic - the taste for comfortable textiles like velvets, silks or even 100-percent cotton. He likes a soft bedspread and always a king-sized bed. Creature comforts are fundamental.

Gemini

(May 21-June 21)

Planet: Mercury, god of communication

Metal: Mercury, the messenger god (desire to communicate and experience variety)

Base Element: Air

Scent: Lavender

Flower: Lily

Color: Yellow and Green

Stone: Aquamarine

The Gemini is happy, intelligent and talkative, exuding a happy-go-lucky quality. Constant change is the state of his home decor. Colors will change. Even the furniture - perhaps on wheels - will be moved around frequently. This penchant for re-arranging reflects a childish spirit who loves everything that he can move and manipulate. As a result, his furniture is generally light, practical, and preferably on wheels.

As you can imagine, he adores iridescent color that changes with every light. Yellow is one of his favorite shades. He is happiest hosting informal gatherings in his home. Great conversations at happy hour will keep Gemini amused for hours.

Likewise, one of the Gemini's favorite places is near the telephone. Of course! Charming and captivating, talking comes natural to Gemini and here he spends hours and hours communicating with family and friends. As a result, he always seems to know everything that is going on.

If Gemini has Virgo in the Fourth House, he probably will have a tendency to clutter - piles of magazines and newspapers are the norm in his household.

Cancer

(June 22-July 22)

Planet: Moon, associated with Diana, protector of the night
(desire to cocoon, protect, make a safe home and reflect the light of others)
Metal: Silver
Base Element: Water
Scent: Jasmine or rose
Flower: Lily or white rose
Color: Antique rose, pearl and silver
Stone: Pearl, emerald and moonstone

Cancer is the Fourth House, concerned with the home. With the Moon as his planet,
Cancer is maternal. Think chocolate-chip cookies baking in the oven and rooms filled with cozy
spaces chock-full of special mementos. Framed pictures of family and loved ones decorate every room
and overall background tones are light grey, pearl beige and white.

Lots of pillows on the sofa and soft rugs on the floor are other Cancer preferences.
Anything but hard-edged contemporary here! A hammock on the patio or a rocking chair
in the living room would be natural selections for Cancer.

With Libra in the Fourth House - draperies will likely be made of lace. Filtered light comes in
through lace-covered windows and for Cancer there is never too much light. The Libra's influence
also brings out Cancer's tendency toward romanticism through candlelight dinners perhaps followed
by a slow dance in the living room. Nearby, always, are lovely roses displayed in a silver
or crystal vase.

Leo

(July 23-August 22)

Planet: Sun, the god Apollo (desire to shine and be the center of attention)

Metal: Gold

Base Element: Fire

Scent: Citrus

Flower: Sunflowers and marigolds

Color: Yellow and gold

Stone: Diamond and ruby

Holding his head high, the mighty lion rules his jungle home. The child born under the sign of the lion has similar authority in his own home. With a keen sense of style and a zest for life, Leo will have somehow impacted his image into every room with furnishings that reflect the elegance and comfort he loves. Don't be surprised to see the family crest on display as Leo creates his very own "castle." Lovely chandeliers and candlesticks will also be part of the ambiance because this is the place where he shines. His planet is the sun and Leo loves the tones of orange and gold, manifested in gold hardware, china patterns, and picture frames.

And speaking of pictures, only the best signed originals meet his standard. This desire for exclusivity is one of Leo's major characteristics. Everything that belongs to Leo has to make him stand apart from other mere mortals.

Leo usually has a keen ability to organize others and he loves to "rule" in his own living room, quite comfortably seated on his special chair, from which he can receive and advise his friends. The living room (preferably with a fireplace) and the bedroom are his favorite places in his "kingdom".

Virgo

(August 23-September 22)

Planet: Mercury, the messenger god (desire for details and precision)

Metal: Mercury

Base Element: Earth

Scent: Wood, sandal wood and lavender

Flower: Cornflower

Color: Navy blue, white and ochre

Stone: Onyx

Virgo values order and neatness over comfort. Furniture with lots of drawers and divisions helps him maintain this order. The Virgo's home is definitely the cleanest of the Zodiac and also the most organized - ready for *Architectural Digest* to dissect and admire.

The child born under the sign of Virgo is naturally attracted to neutral tones, especially ochres, taupes and cinnamons. These tones are naturally easier to keep clean - and, of course, they are also the earthtones, representative of his element, the earth. Light natural woods and rustic or ethnic furnishings are his favorite, with fabrics and rugs in natural fibers.

The Virgo's favorite place is the yard or garden, where he loves to plant flowers. If you are ever invited into his impeccable house, you will likely see a selection of interesting potted plants! Critical analysis is a strong Virgo trait - even about who may or may not be invited into his home. So if you are invited, you should consider yourself very lucky to have passed the Virgo's discriminating scrutiny!

Virgo adores music, especially the classics featuring violin and piano. His house will probably have a space for meditation, preferably in blue tones.

Libra

(September 23-October 23)

Planet: Venus, goddess of love (desire for harmony and balance)

Metal: Copper

Base Element: Air

Scent: Florals, especially rose

Color: Pastel blue, pink and green

Stone: Sapphire and jade

Harmony and balance are the quintessential elements in every area of the Libra's home.

Born under the sign of the scale, and with its planet being Venus, the child of Libra is characterized by his traits of sympathy, harmony and above all, hospitality.

Always concerned with others and the most social sign of the Zodiac, he will welcome guests with well-chosen dinnerware, linens and crystals. Libra is naturally tuned to the aesthetic and knows instinctively how to harmonize colors, forms and volumes better than any other sign in the Zodiac.

He likes soft, pastel tones including pink, green, and blue. He loves copper objects (copper being the metal associated with Venus) but he also favors bronze, especially in the form of sculptures.

Every Libra is fascinated by the Greek aesthetic and prefers a unified look without mixing a lot of colors and styles. Even if he opts for furniture with more modern lines, this furniture will always be representative of classic modernism such as the work of Le Corbusier or Mies van der Rohe.

Art objects are the very passion of Libras who, if given a choice, will always invest in an artistic piece rather than any mundane purchase such as replacing the chipped mirror in the bathroom.

Libras are especially attuned to the foyer and living room since these are key areas associated with entertaining. Libra's eternal desire to make others happy can be manifested in many ways in the home. By offering comfort and a pleasant evening, or even by presenting unexpected gifts.

Scorpio

(October 24-November 21)

Planet: Pluto, god of the underworld (desire to bring new life from old)

Metal: Iron and steel

Base Element: Water

Scent: Pine and citrus

Colors: Deep red and black

Stone: Topaz and opal

Mysterious secrets, perhaps with a dark side, and sheer sensuality are characteristics of Scorpio.

These traits will manifest themselves throughout the home in deep, rich tones. And there will always be at least one secret place! Likewise, Scorpios themselves are intense, sensual and possessive.

Their planet, Pluto, is indeed a very dark place, and this explains the Scorpio's extreme sensibility to light. As a result, they surround themselves with lamps and window treatments that allow only indirect light, which is necessary to protect their sensitive eyes and guarantee an erotic ambiance.

When it comes to colors, black, purple and dark tones have a special place in the Scorpio home.

They prefer using these as contrasts with strong colors such as dark green, bright red, or navy blue. These peculiar colors are frequently combined with modern furniture and objects of art with an exotic design. Strong and sensual scents of natural musk oil or sandal wood incense excite the Scorpio because Scorpio corresponds to the nasal passages and the genital organs in the human body.

The bedroom is where Scorpio feels most at home. There he can exercise all of his sensuality. He also likes the bathroom, which is the most intimate room. Scorpio will often transform the bathroom into a modern ambiance by using strong colors.

Scorpios love privacy and intimacy so they always have locked drawers, armoires with keys and trunks where they keep their "secrets." When you go into a Scorpio house you feel like staying until you decipher all the mysteries that seem to discover in each corner.

Sagittarius

(November 22-December 21)

Planet: Jupiter, king of the gods (desire to expand and reach out)
Metal: Tin
Base Element: Fire
Scent: Citrus and jasmine
Flower: Carnation
Colors: Royal blue and purple
Stone: Topaz

Sagittarius is a natural optimist, enthusiastic and positive, exuding an intense desire to be connected with the rest of the world. He also has an intense fear of enclosed spaces. Give him a room with a view so he can enjoy observing what is going on through his own personal window on the world.

He prefers large, open spaces in cool colors, and lots of wood - especially in the study or the room where he often meditates. Jupiter, which is related with the highest part of the mind, is his planet and that is why you will probably find the intellectual Sagittarius pondering philosophy or seeking universal truth.

The need for change combined with an intense curiosity about what is going on in the world leads Sagittarius to travel and his home will have a place to display souvenirs from his many trips. When he is forced to stay home, he reads, surfs the Internet or watches television to satisfy this curiosity.

Large windows, skylights, landscape photography or paintings - anything that gives him the sensation of being outdoors will please Sagittarius. He is quite content looking at these beautiful things which often trigger optimistic dreams.

Capricorn

(December 22-January 19)

Planet: Saturn, god of time (desire to control, manage and conserve)
Metal: Lead and silver
Base Element: Earth
Scent: Pine and other woods
Flower: Ivy and pansy
Color: Grey and beige
Stone: Turquoise and amethyst

The child of Capricorn is persistent, serious, very hard working, and his home always reflects these personal characteristics. Due to his penchant for long-term planning he will spend a little more to assure the best quality materials that will last for a very long time. Since he loves continuity and security, this will enable him to go through the years without having to change any of his furnishings.

Typical preferences would be Colonial construction, neutral colors and traditional furniture. His favorite materials are the natural textiles and traditional woods such as mahogany or rosewood. But the most important thing is that the decoration and design of his home is a subtle indication to all guests of the prosperity and professional success of the owner. Special mementos for a trip, for example, will be on display to demonstrate his achievement.

Music is important to Capricorn, often used to cheer him up or calm him down. Day after day the Capricorn accumulates items they feel are necessary. Classical objects like metal sculptures would be typical as would clocks - a constant reminder that everything accumulated must last for a long, long time. Above all, this home needs to be cost-effective!

Aquarius

(January 20-February 18)

Planet: Uranus, god of heaven (desire to innovate, change something for betterment of all)

Metal: Aluminum and lead

Base Element: Air

Scent: Exotics, woods and lavender

Flower: Orchid

Colors: Turquoise

Stone: Aquamarine

Intense, independent, extravagant and impulsive are traits of the Aquarius, who always seems to stand out from the crowd. His home, too, must be strikingly special. Why wait for the future? The future is now! You will immediately notice that Aquarius has all the latest audio and video equipment and shiny metal objects with futuristic design.

Uranus, his planet, is electric by nature. The Aquarius personality is quick to anger - and almost as quick to calm down. Extremely intense, he prefers intense colors featuring abstract motifs and strong contrast.

Colors are selected to enhance his collection of modern objects and to show them off. A favorite way to pass the time in his home includes long discussions about humanitarian ideals. Aquarius are also very authoritarian, including their ideas about decorating, and when it is so clear to them that they are "right," they simply don't understand how others do not agree with them.

An Aquarius feels perfectly at home when he is surrounded with contemporary objects and a lot of friends. He loves entertaining, but hates the clean-up, so he prefers a home that features easy maintenance.

option, then frequently we will design a custom built-in that accommodates the configuration of the wall.

P erla Lichi Design was once commissioned to create interiors for an apartment unit in a prestigious beach front enclave in Fort Lauderdale. This particular unit would serve as the residence for a semi-retired couple who wanted a space where both they and their grandchildren would feel at home. Although downsizing, these empty nesters wanted to step up to a more luxurious lifestyle for their golden years.

Interior design is first and foremost the proper organization of interior spaces to enhance a lifestyle. This often means overcoming certain problems while highlighting each room's strong points. In this case, living areas were small with little or no architectural interest. On the positive side, the apartment's Eastern exposure afforded views of South Florida's most magnificent coastal scenery. By addressing these realities, we were able to achieve the most appropriate and beautiful aesthetic.

Living space in the 22nd floor unit was just 2,200 square feet, and we were pressed to provide the functionality that our client needed and at the same time create a feeling of relaxed spaciousness. Custom cabinetry came to the rescue, in the living, dining and media rooms, tied together with crown moldings stained in a mahogany finish. Mirrors expanded the space visually while enhancing its beachfront ambiance by introducing reflected images of magnificent coastal views.

"The exterior architecture of many new high rises often results in rooms that have odd-angles. When we are faced with such angles, we first analyze whether or not to alter the floor plan to smooth out or square off these angles."

A wonderful aspect of interior design is our ability to take the imperfections as they come and camouflage or correct them. Come to think of it, interior design is really a lot like make-up. Our tools consists of paint and wallpaper, fabric, carpets and rugs, lighting and furniture, among many other things, with which we can create beautiful environments.

Without a doubt one of the most cost-effective and efficient options is that of custom built-ins. The modern home is not complete without an entertainment center. Adding additional storage is a constant, on-going request. Clients have shopped until they dropped and failed to find furniture that fits a particular space.

Custom built-ins solve these and other design problems at both ends of the spectrum. They can maximize the use of any space, no matter how odd the angles may be. And, they can also be used to enhance very plain rooms that are completely devoid of architectural detailing.

The exterior architecture of many new high rises often results in rooms that have odd-angles. When we are faced with such angles, we first analyze whether or not to alter the floor plan to smooth out or square off these angles. If this is not an

"The expenditure of 30 or 40 thousand dollars for a new car — not only once in their lives but every few years — is considered the norm. Yet making this type of investment for beautiful home interiors still raises eyebrows."

Working With a Rough Jewel

Design Functions as a Problem Solver

Nothing in life is perfect. Priceless jewels require the stone cutter's painstaking skill to release their true beauty, and minor flaws are still almost always inevitable. A beautiful fashion model, admired for the symmetry of her face, uses eyeliner, mascara and eye shadows to enhance her eyes; a make-up base plus powder, blush and rouge to add contour. And she is most conscious of how she is "lit" when photographed, knowing that lighting can transform her image from siren to swan.

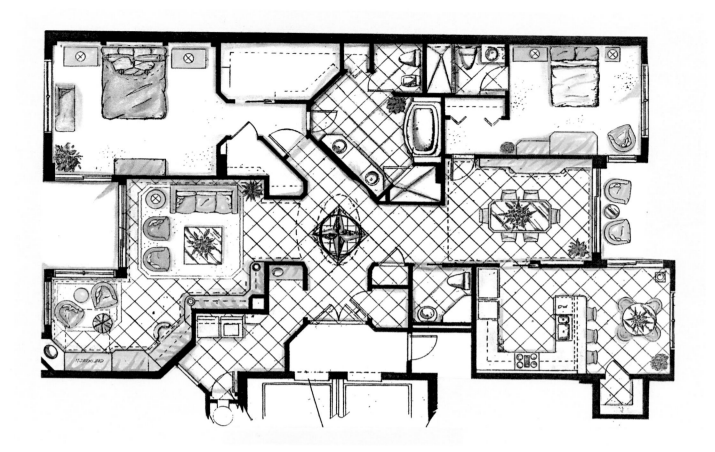

Floor Plan

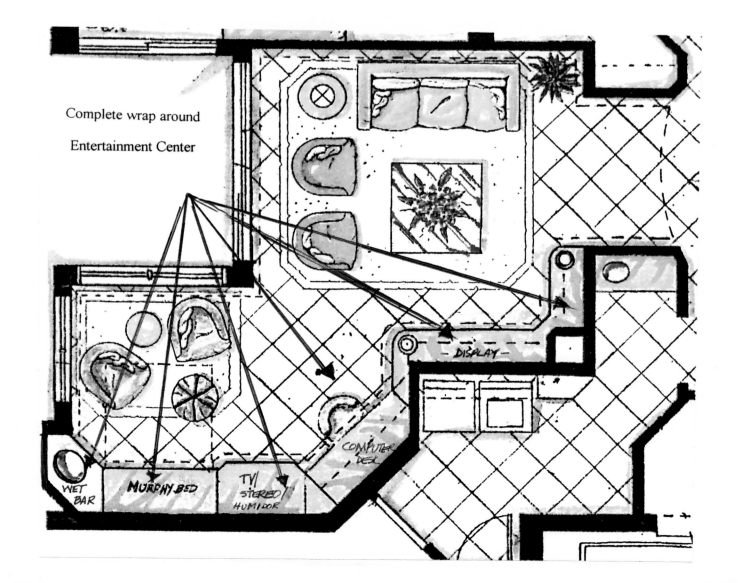

Complete wrap around

Entertainment Center

DISPLAY

COMPUTER DESK

WET BAR

MURPHY BED

TV/ STEREO/ HUMIDOR

Moldings throughout and elaborate columns such as those framing the sofa are used as architectural elements to visually expand the living spaces in the 22nd floor residence. Several more strategically placed decorative columns were added for much-needed architectural interest in otherwise plain, rectangular rooms.

Exterior architecture of both towers showcases the understated elegance of this seaside resort community. This unit, while relatively small compared to the larger models, now incorporates many custom elements that maximize use of every inch of the 2,200-square-foot space. This couple enjoys a magnificent, carefree seaside home with all the amenities of a fine hotel.

At another high rise, gaining maximum efficiency out of small space was a high priority. This, combined with a very odd wall angle, left us only one choice: custom built-ins. Here, we created a large unit that housed a wet bar, storage, entertainment center and even a Murphy-style bed! Let me provide one final example of the flexibility of custom built-ins. Clients recently requested a guest room in their vacation home that would double as a sitting room. Plus, they wanted the room to be versatile enough to accommodate one or two guests comfortably. Our solution was to create a custom unit, which housed two single Murphy-style beds. It worked beautifully.

"Custom built-ins solve design problems at both ends of the spectrum. They can maximize the use of any space, no matter how odd the angles may be. And, they can also be used to enhance very plain rooms that are completely devoid of architectural detailing."

CUSTOM ENTERTAINMENT CENTER

CUSTOM DINING ROOM BUFFET

"Here is the magnificent, multi-purpose built-in wall unit, based on the renderings shown on the previous page."

Design as an Investment
Remodeling for Resale

Everyone knows that if you want to sell your property, you need to spruce it up a bit for potential buyers. But it is surprising that more people don't realize an investment in professional interior design almost always means a quicker sale and an almost immediate return on their investment.

Let me cite two clients who are also savvy real estate investors.

This ugly duckling single family home sat on the market for more than two years. With its long, dark kitchen, master bath the size of a postage stamp and many other problems, it really looked shabby. At the same time, it was located in a prime waterfront location among the most prestigious neighborhoods in downtown Fort Lauderdale.

My clients, both classical musicians, were experienced real estate investors, originally from Greensboro, North Carolina, where they had renovated other homes. They quickly became active in the local South Florida real estate market and saw investment possibilities in buying and upgrading this particular property.

Previous owners of the home had renovated the great room with a high-beamed ceiling and plenty of light. My clients devised a remodeling plan that included the addition of a master bedroom suite and a kitchen/family room. Everything was gutted but the slab from the former tiny kitchen and main bedroom and more than 1,000 square feet of living space added. French doors and windows plus triple-gabled roofs gave the renovated house the Key West character the owners sought.

"My clients purchased the house and after investing in remodeling and upgrades, sold it within a year of living there for $1 million plus ."

Inside, the Key West style was continued in a palette of beachside colors on faux painted walls, unpolished travertine flooring, and moldings.

A mirrored niche wall was added in the new master bedroom suite, where moldings were added to the impressive triple-tray ceiling. The wall in the living area of the great room was also created as a display unit. The great room was divided by furniture groupings, including dining table and chairs. A huge mirror was installed as an illusionary devise to divert the eyes from the two doorways to reflect the view from certain angles.

My clients purchased the house, and after investing in remodeling and upgrades, they sold it within a year of living there for $1 million plus — making about 30 percent on their investment. In any business, that's certainly a nice return on your money.

Another investor/client purchased two units that were combined into one magnificent oceanside penthouse. The floor plan was then altered to create two distinct suites with baths and a master bedroom with sitting area, facing the ocean. He wanted the interior decoration to have such an impact that the "right" buyer would love everything and want to move right in. He specified elegant overall

"They made about 30 percent on their investment. In any business, that's certainly a nice return on your money."

styling with slight masculine flavor, which the designers translated into this universally appealing masterpiece for maximum salability.

Aware that this "right buyer" would be sophisticated, worldly and a frequent entertainer, our designers went to work to create the necessary living environment.

Since there were few walls, custom built-ins and architectural millwork helped to delineate the spaces. A multi-coffered living room soffit and a two-step dining room soffit are highlighted with mahogany crown moldings. Built-in cabinetry and millwork include a room divider to create a separate card area and built-in media center/home theater.

As part of the living room, the home theater houses a large-screen TV and state-of-the-art audio/video equipment. Built-in cabinetry wraps the odd wall shape. A custom sofa mirrors this shape and affords an unobstructed view. Other built-ins match the rich cherry color of the magnificent custom unit done in Neoclassical carved wood styling.

"Investing in professional interior design to show a new property to its fullest potential or to remodel an existing property adds immediate cache that you will almost certainly enjoy in two distinct ways."

The spacious kitchen was created for use by professional caterers with all the amenities and very ample workspace. The walk-in butler's pantry features the same granite counter and backsplash as the main kitchen. Cabinets were stained to coordinate with built-ins throughout the residence. A cafe-type casual dining area was created so the floor-to-ceiling view would not be obstructed – an essential ingredient in high-rise living.

Other highlights include richly appointed baths, luxurious bedrooms, always with attention to comfortable and carefree living demanded by this clientele.

My client purchased the two penthouses and invested another $250,000 for the turnkey interior design with the modifications described above. Within a few months a buyer was willing to pay the price that netted the investor 25 to 30 percent return.

"You will of course enjoy living in the beautiful interiors yourself. Second, you will be able to increase your bottom line in the most expeditious manner when you decide to sell."

"Today people are looking for more than color coordination. They are seeking peace and comfort that comes from being surrounded with elements of good design."

As my own design practice has increased, I have invested in real estate in new developments. In my case, investing in interior design reaps dual benefits. I can show this newly designed apartment as a model to new buyers so they will commission Perla Lichi Design to design their unit. At the same time, this "model" is always for sale and often sells immediately after we hold our "grand opening" party for realtors and potential buyers.

You probably never thought of interior design in these terms, but I could cite example after example. Investing in professional interior design to show a new property to its fullest potential or to remodel an existing property adds immedizate cache that you will almost certainly enjoy in two distinct ways. You will, of course, enjoy living in the beautiful interiors yourself. Second, you will be able to increase your bottom line in the most expeditious manner when you decide to sell.

"Come to think of it, interior design
is really a lot like make-up. Our tools consist
of paint and wallpaper, fabric, carpets and
rugs, lighting, furniture and
accessories, with which we create
beautiful environments."

How to Work With a Designer

What to Expect and What Not to Expect

Interior designers often compare their work to that of a good therapist. First, identify the client's problems, and then apply professional techniques to arrive at "healthy" solutions. While I am certainly not a doctor, I do approach each project with the goal of providing my clients with happy, nurturing environments.

"Your home is the place where your dreams can come true. The right interior designer has the ability to bring your project to completion in the most expeditious manner and with the most professional results."

I know that most professional designers, including myself, realize just how involved we become with our clients. We get to know about their habits, their children, and their children's habits. As the relationship grows, we become acutely aware of their subtle likes and dislikes. At the same time, we are learning about their color and style preferences, or, in my case, studying their astrological signs. After all, we are creating their living environment and it is impossible to do so successfully without this knowledge.

There are many things to be considered when selecting a designer, and there are as many styles of designers as there are individuals working in this profession. As this chapter indicates, I want to steer you away from false expectations. If you are building a new house, I think it is a good idea to select your interior designer at the same time you select your architect, builder and landscape architect. This "team" will work together to avoid common design problems such as problem traffic corridors or misplaced doors and windows, to name only a few.

You need to shop around for a designer exactly the same way you would select any professional. Have a fairly clear idea in mind about what you want to accomplish, when, and what your budget limitations are. Schedule an appointment and conduct an interview. Check references and credentials. And always ask for the names of recent clients whom you may call for reference. If possible, actually visit a job site to see some of the results for yourself.

There are many ways designers work. Some work on a "cost plus" basis where they charge a commission on all items purchased. Others work on an hourly rate and there are even designers who work on a flat fee basis. That all will depend on your needs as well as each designer's individual style of working. More important than anything is the need to feel comfortable with your designer so you will not be hesitant to bring up anything regarding your job — no matter how insignificant it may seem to you. It is also essential to have total confidence in your designer's professionalism. Each client certainly wants to reap all the benefits of their designer's training and experience. Yet ironically, one of the major complaints I hear from designers is that clients will not allow them to work to the best of their ability. If you don't have this level of confidence and trust, then I don't think you will have a successful experience, and you should continue to look for a designer.

While researching this chapter, I realized that the subject has been covered many times before, but in a rather stiff or "textbooky" way — certainly not my style. I think there are many unspoken realities about interior design, and that making people more aware of at least some of them would result in infinitely improved client/designer relationships. Over the years my experiences have run the gamut from huge disappointments and outright rage to wonderful moments of humor with a few periods of sheer bliss thrown in for good measure.

In addition to sharing my experiences, I decided to poll other designers about what clients should expect from their designer and what they should not expect. Here are some of their thoughts:

"Design installations do not always go as planned, and Murphy's Law seems to be especially active on certain jobs. When problems happen, as they almost always do, the clients just need to relax and realize this is simply part of the process. Allow us to do our job — which includes handling such snafus."

"Delivery is an extra charge."

"The client should realize that as a successful interior designer who wants to stay in business, I am probably working with several clients at the same time — not just them! If the client were to absorb all of my time, they would need to pay a very huge fee indeed! And since they probably do not want to pay such a fee, he or she needs to respect me as a business person who needs more than one client!"

"The client should find a decorator who will listen to their needs and respond to their tastes. It is the client's house — not the decorator's. As a designer, I am appalled by the number of decorators who do projects as they would like, not thinking about the client's tastes or preferences."

"If the client already has some nice pieces, then we should use them."

"If you are building a new house, I think it is a good idea to select your interior designer at the same time you select your architect, builder and landscape architect."

76

"A lot of communication with each client is essential. Clients need and deserve our attention."

"Once a client has requested design work, the designer should develop solutions and make a presentation quickly, within two weeks or three at most, and then proceed just as quickly as possible with the work. Of course, this depends entirely on the vendors that are selected."

"This is very psychological work, so designers must understand each client and be very, very patient with them."

"Don't expect that the designer will insist that everything will be only her/his taste. A good designer should respect the client and the design should reflect the client's tastes. Also, a good designer will incorporate the client's prized possessions. Everything does not have to be discarded!"

Are you a chef? Have you ever baked a cake from scratch? The total number of ingredients in a cake is nine or perhaps ten different items at most that must be accurately measured, then mixed in a certain way. Next you fill the cake pan and bake (again using a very precise temperature). Next you allow the cake to cool and add frosting when appropriate. Now compare interior design to the process of baking. An average living room can incorporate hundreds of different "ingredients." Each item requires a different skilled craftsman or vendor. With interior design we have many people to deal with as well as a most diverse range of products and materials. Our vendors are our lifeblood and our relationship with them – as you can well imagine – is precious. Since many of these are skilled artisans themselves, they often have a creative, artistic nature, which requires special nurturing because we always want their very best efforts on behalf of our valued clients. Location and climate conditions of the job site are just small variables in the daily routine of the average interior designer. Since your project is your primary concern, you want the maximum results for the best price. Your home is the place where your dreams can come true. The right interior designer has the ability to bring your project to completion in the most expeditious manner and with the most professional results.

Fulfilling Those Lifelong Dreams

Downsizing for the Golden Years

How does one let go of a lifetime of memories? This is definitely not an easy step to take. And yet it comprises only one small part of the trauma of facing that it is no longer possible to maintain the family home. Since the majority of my work is in South Florida, many of my clients are downsizing and

relocating from other states. They have been frequent visitors to Florida over the years, but there's still a large psychological bridge to cross when it comes to relocating permanently. Often, this is combined with other major life changes, including children leaving home, retirement, or the illness and the death of a spouse.

Some general advice is that you do not need to let go of the memories. They will always be with you. And a good way to ensure this is by taking lots of photos of the family home, with close-ups of especially beloved furnishings, art and accessories. Organize all of these photos in an album. Besides creating a wonderful keepsake, this also becomes a practical tool that can help you discuss with others – including your designer – what to keep and what not to keep while you are planning your new environment.

Another rule of thumb is not to design your new living environment for the few weeks when your children and grandchildren may be visiting. Plan for them, to be sure, but don't maintain empty rooms that will just make you miss them even more. The key for today's living in smaller spaces is to create dual-purpose rooms that will be used and enjoyed throughout the year.

The third piece of advice is to look on this step in your life as a great new adventure. It can actually serve to mark a new beginning that will help you adjust to life's changes. If you approach it with this attitude, as the old adage says, perhaps the best is yet to come!

I want to share my experience with some "downsizers" who allowed sound design

"Russian artist Yuri was commissioned to create a bold, tropical scene on the kitchen wall. As a special personal touch, the names of family members are incorporated into the painting, including that of their beloved dog, Champagne."

advice to help them through this important and often traumatic milestone.

Our clients moved from a very large apartment in New York City with four bedrooms, three bathrooms and 13 closets into a smaller, 1,680 square foot ocean side condominium on the 23rd floor of a brand new high rise. The husband, an investment banker, was retiring after 32 years and their two grown children were definitely leaving the nest for college and marriage.

In a way, this couple was easier to design for than most downsizers because they wanted a fresh start and had already decided to leave most of their furniture behind. They still had a large art collection, however, and in addition to creating their "dream getaway" they instructed us to "make use of every inch" to incorporate additional storage space. Another plus was the fact that they purchased their unit "pre-construction" and hired us early so we could work together to determine any changes we might want to make before our installation began. One such alteration involved switching the function of two areas. What the builder had determined was to be the dining room would better serve the clients as a sitting room. This required a slight change in electrical wiring so the new dining area could accommodate a chandelier.

Our design team watched while the clients looked through various photographs and magazines and it soon became apparent that they were both drawn to a contemporary deco style. By getting to know this couple better, we also realized that they had a wonderful zest for life and a great sense of humor.

Here are some exceptional features of their new home:

• Two wooden pillars were installed to mark the small foyer area. No one could decide which way these tapered

"This all new 'dream' apartment afforded our clients a chance to create every amenity they had always wanted. They loved the results and to celebrate hosted a unique party for the entire Perla Lichi Design team with the theme of a theatre opening."

wooden pillars looked best. As a spur-of-the-moment compromise that everyone loved — one was placed up, one down — which reflects the subtle, whimsical flavor of the entire apartment — and themselves.

• A drop-down "bar" in the sitting room resembles "wall art" when not in use. This is a wonderful use of space in a small area. In the same sitting room, "end tables" that flank the sofa open from the top to double as deep storage cabinets.

• The wife, an avid collector of unusual creative items from around the world, found a group of ceramic lizards during her travels to the Southwest that needed a "home" in the new apartment. Russian artist Yuri was commissioned to create a bold, tropical scene on the kitchen wall. As a special personal touch, the names of the family members are incorporated into the painting, including that of their beloved dog, "Champagne." Note how happy the ceramic lizards are in their new environment!

• Her computer desk (which doubles as a server) is placed in front of this colorful mural in the kitchen.

• The designer ensured maximum use of the apartment's wonderful views through use of mirrors — even in the bathrooms.

• A queen Murphy-style bed conveniently turns the office into a guest room.

• The unusual glass deco carved shower door, which can be uniquely lit, is a commissioned work of art.

• The apartment is wired throughout for custom sound and lighting effects with every room capable of receiving independently of the other rooms. All lighting is on dimmers.

• Thirty small soffit halogen lights are installed around the main living areas for dramatic and practical lighting effects.

• Custom built-ins throughout the apartment instead of walls help delineate the different living spaces. The use of white-washed maple wood for crown moldings, decorative effects, and custom cabinetry creates a harmonious look that flows from room to room.

This all new "dream" apartment afforded this couple a chance to create every amenity they had always wanted. They loved the results and to celebrate hosted a unique party for the entire Perla Lichi Design team with the theme of a theatre opening.

"By getting to know this couple better,
we also realized that they had a wonderful
zest for life and a great sense of humor."

Castles in the Air

Condominium Living

There is nothing quite so glamorous as living in a high-rise condominium with a magnificent ocean view. Yes, instead of dreaming about a house in the suburbs, many South Floridians are dreaming of owning their own "castle in the air."

High-rise decorating always focuses on one key aspect: The View. We always do everything possible to maximize this wonderful aesthetic aspect such as strategic positioning of mirrors and placement of seating groups. We will often rethink space planning in order to provide unobstructed vistas of magnificent views and, if possible, let this be part of the first impression — visible from the moment a person enters the residence through the front door.

Corporate Executive from Chicago

This couple wanted maximum use out of each room and a rich, opulent ambiance.

This apartment reflects the client's desire for a rich, Neoclassical ambiance. They wanted texture, not color; opulence, not glitz. This was achieved with masterful combining of marble, alabaster, crackle finishes, woods, leafing and glass that flows throughout the residence like good karma. Setting this tone immediately is a silver leaf and beveled cut glass and iron entry door and illuminated alabaster columns that flank the foyer console, enhanced all around with tromp l'oeil and other faux effects.

A daytime sitting room that doubles as a guest room reflects the client's African-American heritage. Unique fabrics, objets d'art, wallpaper border at ceiling height and tropical fan are highlights, and twin Murphy-style beds allow for flexible entertaining: one or two guests.

The great room custom built-in unit incorporates a large-screen TV and additional screens for watching several stations at once. An autonomous den was created with a custom built-in divider with ornate, decorative columns that define recessed niche shelves. Niche lighting emphasizes collectibles. Crackle finish on custom built-ins adds a subtle element of tone and texture. Note the carved wood lion's head motif details that add finishing touch of elegance. Crown molding ties this area with adjacent rooms.

The master bedroom and bath reflect the look of the entire residence. Through use of mirrored walls around the tub, the bathroom appears larger than it actually is. Light, natural tones work together with the footprint creating ideal comfort, convenience and functionality. The lit, etched-glass privacy panel also doubles as a "night light."

"Setting this tone immediately is a
silver leaf and beveled cut glass and iron entry door
and illuminated alabaster columns that flank the foyer
console, enhanced all around with tromp l'oeil and
other faux effects."

"Through the use of mirrored walls around the tub, the bathroom appears larger than it actually is. The lit, etched-glass privacy panel also doubles as a night light."

Colombians Prefer Formal Sophistication

This VIP couple from Bogota, Colombia, knew they would often find themselves entertaining VIP guests in their Fort Lauderdale vacation getaway. They wanted an opulent, elegant look similar to the surroundings they were used to in their South American home. They also thought that a formal decor would provide the most appropriate ambiance for their museum-quality collection of antiques, bronzes, and tapestries.

One of their stated preferences was for the designer to create a dramatic statement in the elevator lobby. They wanted people to say "Wow!" as soon as they got off the elevator. Keeping in mind the scope and range of their furnishings and collectibles, we created a very dramatic red-and-gold lobby. With its Oriental influence, the lobby successfully sets the desired tone and definite "Wows" are heard from almost everyone who sees it. If guests happen to look up, they'll also admire the crowning effect of a gilded dome-shaped ceiling and a crystal chandelier. Built-in cabinetry provided a key element in the design scheme. Here, however, the wooden cabinets, cupboards and shelves, combined with built-in wall units, serve as a backdrop for displaying all of the magnificent pieces of an extensive art collection. To contribute to the desired effect of luxe and opulence, walls were faux finished in soft, pastel tones. Tapestry fabrics provide contrast to the authentic antique rugs on the floors.

Pattern on pattern from the rich tapestry and antique rugs was complemented by the use of classically patterned upholstery and decorative pillows. Note, also, the more formal window treatments that were developed for this residence, utilizing swags, fringes, and layering, such as one might see in a European castle.

"Pattern on pattern from the rich tapestry and antique rugs was complemented by the use of classically patterned upholstery and decorative pillows."

"One of their stated preferences was for the designer to create a dramatic statement in the elevator lobby. They wanted people to say 'wow' as soon as they got off the elevator."

"For this spectacular bathroom, designed to appeal to upscale buyers
we created a wall behind the tub to camouflage a sports shower behind.
The glass blocks still allow natural light to flow through the room. Potential
buyers liked this so much that it was incorporated as a builder's upgrade."

Model Merchandising
Working with Builders and Developers

Builders and developers understand that in order to sell their properties, they need to entice potential buyers with all the benefits they have to offer. And the best way show off a property to best advantage is to provide furnished models – often a variety of models – that buyers can wander through and dream about as if it were their own residence.

Interior design and real estate are therefore close partners in creating interiors that "sell." When we obtain such commissions, we first learn as much as we can about the target market. Then it becomes vitally important for us to completely understand the spaces that we are designing, beginning with a detailed floor plan. Many times we work hand-in-hand with the builders even before construction begins to suggest certain modifications to the plan when we believe such changes will result in more livable spaces.

In order for you to better understand this process, I have selected two recent examples. The first model was developed for Hispanic first-time buyers at a price range of $105,000 to $125,000. The second model was specifically designed to appeal to professional couples who have rapidly moved up the social scale. Located within a gated community, this model sells for a base price of $450,000.

A Model for First-Time Buyers

The four-bedroom Versailles model with den/option needed to create an immediate impact of importance for this buyer, with the same quality image as if he had paid twice as much for the home. The concept, through interior decor, was that the buyer would walk in and say "Yes!" I can afford all these things I have been dreaming about such as a home office, luxurious window treatments, and entertainment center."

The elongated floor plan with no formal dining room or living room needed visual definition. Our design team knew that a formal dining room was absolutely essential for this market. The designer accomplished this by incorporating faux stone Corinthian columns and arches, leaving a feeling of openness, yet with clear room divisions. The optional den is shown as a home office using a library look with elegant French doors. When the doors are open, this room visually becomes part of the main living area. The family room features a complete entertainment center.

The family room and library feature drywall columns. The designers later applied moldings, trim and cabinetry to these columns to create a custom built-in effect for a minimum cost. The idea was to excite the buyer enough that he would include this as an upgrade and it worked! Almost 90 percent of buyers are taking this option!

"The family room and library feature drywall columns. The designers later applied moldings, trim and cabinetry to these columns to create a custom built-in effect for a minimum cost."

"This attractive home was designed to appeal to second or third-time buyers upgrading to better schools in a better neighborhood that reflects their financial and social success."

A Model for Experienced Buyers

This 4,300 sq. ft. San Rafael model is located in a master-planned community with a championship 18-hole golf course. It was built by a developer specializing in custom home designs who has built more than 2,000 homes in South Florida during the last 25 years. This attractive home was designed to appeal to second or third-time buyers; people upgrading to better schools in a better neighborhood that reflects their financial and social success. Busy professionals with young children and teenagers, they want all of today's latest bells and whistles that they have worked so hard to achieve.

This four-bedroom home with an open floor plan also has a library and family room. When reviewing the plans, images of old-world charm immediately came to mind. The architectural details in the living room and dining room easily lent themselves to a formal and opulent atmosphere, while the master bedroom, with views of the pool area, was perfect for bringing the outdoors inside.

With the use of marble and stone in earth tones, our designers evoked the feeling of a piazza. To achieve the desired formal elegance, trompe l'oeil was applied to recessed niches in the living room and dining room. These not only highlighted the wonderful architectural details but continued to elicit a feeling of being in a villa. Columns, sconces, ornate gold-framed mirrors and unique urns completed the transformation. As in most homes, the family room is the most popular area for informal entertaining. To create a more casual atmosphere while still retaining the overall Mediterranean feeling, a custom built-in entertainment center was accented with columns. A comfortable seating area invites guests to gather and relax.

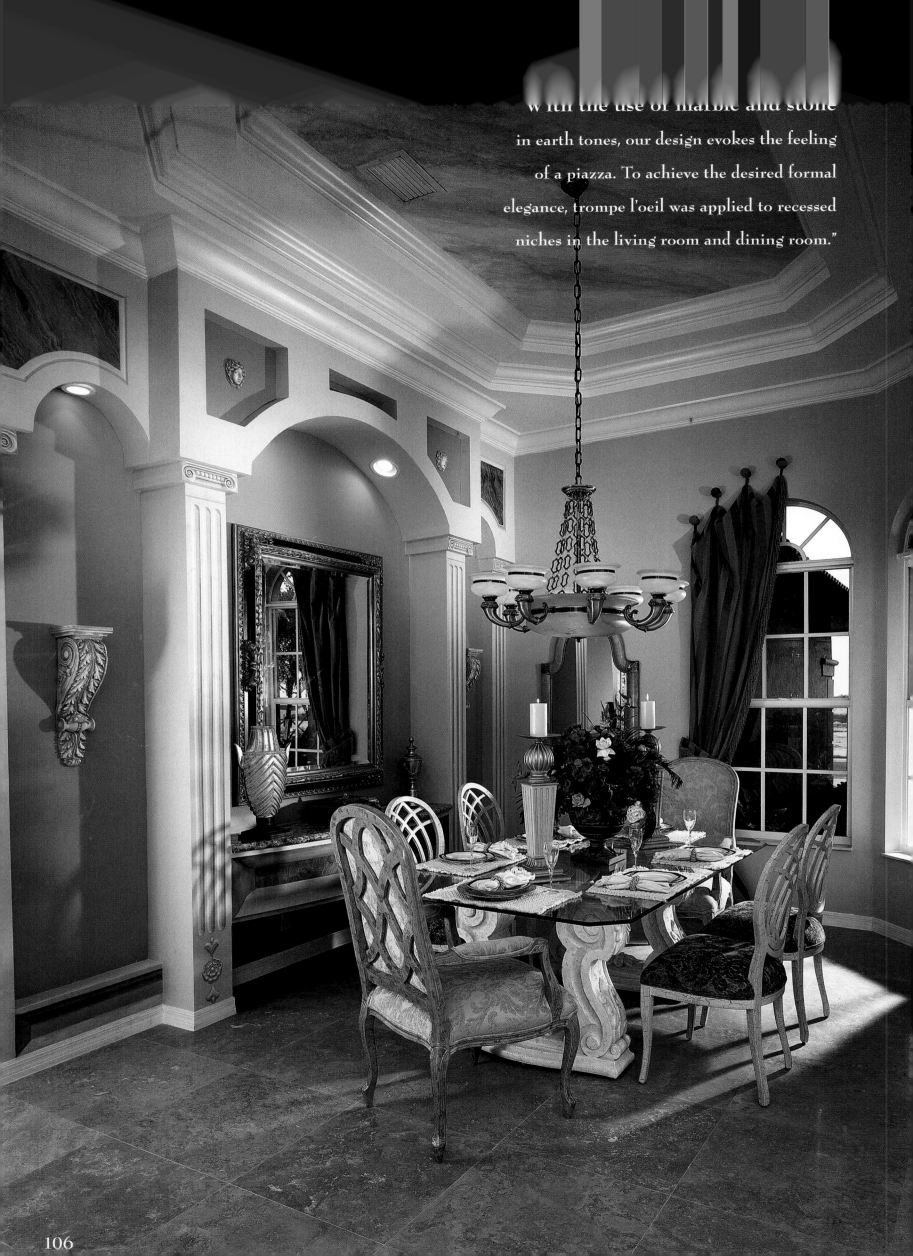

"With the use of marble and stone in earth tones, our design evokes the feeling of a piazza. To achieve the desired formal elegance, trompe l'oeil was applied to recessed niches in the living room and dining room."

The design of the built-in shelving in the family room is carried over into the study. The simple yet elegant desk, plush chair with ottoman, area rug and minimal window treatment all serve to make this room inviting for work or quiet contemplation. The master bedroom suite and its wonderful view of the pool were ideal for creating a lavish, secluded atmosphere, and for maintaining the feeling of being outdoors in an old-world Mediterranean piazza. Two mirror panels installed on either side of the built-in headboard, reflecting the luxurious pool area and beyond, evoke an open-air feeling.

The piazza ambiance was continued in the master bath with the use of marble and stone in earth tones. To camouflage the shower stall behind the tub, we designed a richly textured wall. With the addition of a mirror flanked by columns, a window effect was created. Wall-to-wall mirrors behind both vanities added depth to this sumptuous bath.

The boy's bedroom walls feature an old map, detailed borders, and rich, dark woods for a distinctively masculine look. Columns, a built-in desk and shelving provide the setting fit for any student. In the girl's bedroom, the addition of subtle reds and greens in the borders, bedspread, and window treatment provide a feminine variation on an old-world theme. Custom shelving along the walls becomes the perfect showplace for a doll collection. While preserving the grandeur of the art and architecture of past masters such as Leonardo da Vinci, Perla Lichi Design is racing forward in a new century, painting a new canvas with each new interior design.

What better way to sell property than by making it more livable and beautiful!

A Designer's Life

Definitely Not a Nine-to-Five Endeavor

During my career as a designer I have designed and installed a complete home inside of a convention center in less than a week, created a model (apartment) in a day, done many off-the-cuff live television interviews in both English and Spanish, stood for hours at trade shows, and served on numerous advisory boards and panels. Why do I go to these — and other extremes — to promote my design business?

I believe that a person can be endowed with the greatest talent and ability and yet if we don't share these attributes, nothing happens. That's why I have always been a firm believer in multi-phased marketing. In addition to writing this book, I have created a syndicated decorating advice newspaper column under the title, The Decor Diva® By Perla Lichi.

My standard marketing approach includes four-color advertising — as much as I can afford — in a diverse range of newspapers and magazines and making myself available for personal appearances whenever and wherever possible.

Since I am bilingual, I market to both the American and the Hispanic markets. This has proved especially valuable on Hispanic television shows here in South Florida and throughout South America. It also helps that I am relaxed and natural on camera — as long as I'm talking about my favorite subject, which is interior design.

My company hosts at least five "grand opening" events each year when our design jobs are completed. These cocktail parties are primarily planned to develop the model-merchandising end of our business. My firm also participates in two to three local home shows annually.

Professional associations provide another key to my marketing approach. I have been a professional member of the American Society of Interior Designers (A.S.I.D) for more than 10 years. Since model merchandising is a major part of my business, I have been most active as a board member in the Builders Association of South Florida (BASF). This association sponsors a major competition awards program annually, called South Florida's Best, and Perla Lichi Design has entered more than 20 projects each year for the last three years. We have been gratified by winning gold, silver and platinum awards that are proudly displayed in our showroom as well as on the sites that we have designed. I also joined the Latin Builders Association (LBA) and was deeply honored to be named recipient of this fine organization's 2000 Award for Interior

No return: Use care when ordering custom furnit

Question: I'm distraught. We ordered a custom sofa, but it's just not what we expected.

Now our designer says that because it was custom-made for us, we can't return it. Help please.

Answer: This is a dollars and sense issue. Custom means one-of-a-kind, and once you buy anything that is custom-made, unless it has definite flaws or defects, basically you own it.

First, check the small print in your agreement and your terms.

After delivery, if your objection is strictly that you don't like the way the sofa looks, any disagreement comes down to your relationship with your designer.

Once you buy anything that is custom-made, unless it has definite flaws or defects, basically you own it.

You will have to absorb some of the cost, but sometimes designers can find a place to use a rejected custom item elsewhere and help you find a buyer if you absolutely lo...

Specialists help consumers narrow wallpaper se

Question: I want to have my bedroom re-wallpapered and recently went shopping. What a confusing scene. There must be more than 2,000 sample books with more than 100 pages each. Is there

THE DECOR DIVA

kitchen won't accommodate a bar set-up and doesn't have room for other people when I am doing the last-minute dinner preparations. A wet bar in the living room would be ideal, but where would I put it?

don't like do-it-yo...
people are smar...
the value of the...
paint my house?...
thousand dollars...
rounds of golf in...

Design Company of the Year.

Perla Lichi Design is very receptive to new marketing opportunities, and when we investigate each one, we always look for a way to have our company stand out above the rest.

My life as a designer is definitely not a nine-to-five endeavor. My commitment to my profession even continues while I am on my vacation! Together with my husband, Mario, and our two sons, Adam and Izzy, I take a summer and a winter holiday vacation each year. But you can be sure that while enjoying every minute of our trips, Mom is also taking photos of architecture and design ideas that often have a way of insinuating themselves into my designs when I get back in the studio. Many of these sojourns also turn into "buying trips." When I spot unusual items that are well designed and priced, I ship them back to my design showroom. This allows me to use exotic and hard-to-find furnishings and accessories in my work – another touch that make Perla Lichi designs truly unique.

Here are some highlights of other unique marketing activities over the years:

• Creating a neo-classical interior design motif for Dream Home, a quarter million dollar completely furnished, landscaped house built inside the Miami Beach Convention Center. The project—dubbed "Project Genesis" because it was built in only seven days—was completed just in time to highlight the 54th Annual Miami International Home & Garden Show. We wanted to show people how they could achieve a professional result on their own. The 2,250 sq. ft. home featured three bed-

"You may think this is a living room, but it is actually the sitting area of a real estate office located in a large shopping mall. They sell luxury homes and called on Perla Lichi Design to create just the right ambience for their clients."